To all those who believe & to the friends made along the way.

-Mica

Way up north where aurora lights dance, past icebergs and snowbirds and reindeer that prance. Sits **The North Pole**, a truly **magical place**. A land that's said to transcend our own time and space. This sort of place you won't find on a map, and the journey is long to where worlds overlap.

This land is home to sweet **Silver Belle**, a small little elf with big stories to tell. It's here where she laughs, works and plays, and exploring it all would take several days. Luckily **Silver Belle** knows some secret pathways.

Today her tasks are a bit different than the norm, and the cause of this change was a surprise starting to form. While Santa was busy fine-tuning his **cherry** red sleigh, dear **Mrs. Claus** was getting everything to celebrate this momentous day!

"**Sugar Belle** is out beyond the Peppermint Seas, collecting the sap from the sweet Sugar Snap Trees. While she is away and performing great feats, would you be so kind as to help make these treats?"

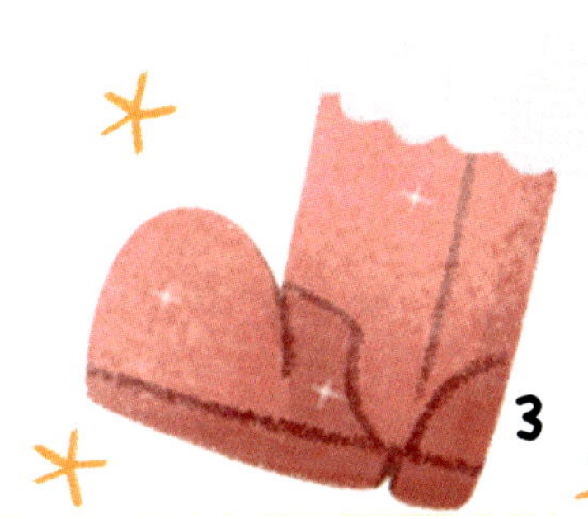

Snickerdoodle, **shortbread**, the list goes on and on. **Chocolate chip**, **peanut butter**, even **apple pecan**. Everyone's favorites were being made, and the pace was blazin'. And yes, they even made **oatmeal** raisin. So many **cookies**, all super **sweet**. **Silver Belle** could hardly wait to try such a special treat! Everything must be done exactly by the book to give these creations their picture-perfect look.

The oven is hot, and ready to go. Now the next step is to stamp out the dough. So many shapes to pick from, so many stencils to try. The tricky part was getting as many out of the dough as possible without anything going awry. Of course no elf is perfect, and there was more than one delicious mistake. But finally they were all resting gently on the trays, all ready to bake.

winter
winter
DEC.
3 4 5 6 7
11 12 13 14
18 19 20
25 26

Mrs. Claus loaded the trays, setting the timers true. All that was left was to patiently wait, and mix the perfect frostings , too. When the cookies were done baking to a crisp golden brown, it seemed like forever until they would cool down. All shapes and sizes, and of all colors and hue. Like big pink polar bears and small snowflakes of blue. How about calico cats, and frosted unicorns too? Maybe some polka dotted penguins paired with the classical peppermint trees. Plus shimmering mermaid tails that splash in the seas! Oh so many sweet ideas, how would one choose? In fact, better to just make them all, in bunches of twos! Batch after batch was ready, how many hundreds did they make?

"Oh how splendid!" **Mrs. Claus** did chime,

"Everything here looks all so sublime! We need to make just one more kind to have things really shine. Turn to the page about gingerbread, Ill let you get started while I go run ahead. Ill be back in two prances, lickidy-quick! I just need to find a way to stall **Mr. Saint Nick**!"

"You leave it to me!" smiled the flour dusted elf, while she reached for the ingredients atop the high shelf.

But while **Silver Belle** was so busy with the measuring and mixing, she didn't even notice when all the gingerbread went all missing!

winter
winter
winter
winter
winter
winter
flour
SPECIAL FORM
STRAWBERRY
PINK SUGAR
"sooo yummy!"
DEC.
4 5 6 7
12 13 14
18 19 20
25 26

“Oh no!”

she exclaimed with a voice full of fright. Without the gingerbreads, this whole surprise wouldn't be just right!

They had been there but a moment ago, and where they were now she just didn't know. The only thing left, was to go out looking. There was still time, while the last batches were cooking. They could not have traveled far, surely someone nearby would know where they all are. So she threw on her coat, and flew out the door. Whatever happened, surely a great adventure was in store.

Her First stop was the stables,led by a crumb trail of sugar and spice

Weaving between jolly snowmen and igloos of ice. She followed it there, where the clues led her inside. Greeted by familiar faces brought a big smile, each friend was adorned in their own unique style.

"I don't suppose you know where I could find a freshly baked snack? You reindeer would eat them all up by the stack. But I doubt the culprits have antlers and hooves, so I better keep looking before something else moves. I'll trust you to keep watch just in case you see anything suspiciously sweet, and I promise when I come back, then I'll give you a treat."
CINCO
MAVERICK
HANK
APOLLO
TESS
CARMEL
SUNDAE
MINDY
PRAIRIE
WILLOW

Now since nothing here seemed out of place, **Silver Belle** had a tough choice to face. All the reindeer were nestled in their comfortable stalls, and nothing seemed to be disturbed at all. Where to next, would the clues lead? **Perhaps Twinkle** could help, with their quick reindeer speed. So off they went through the sparkling snow, just an elf on a mission with a reindeer in tow. Maybe she should follow a familiar sound. For where there was laughter, usually cookies were found.

So it was onto the workshop to go look around. Nothing was here, but magic whirring machines.
With busy workers bustling tirelessly behind the whimsical scenes.

"Hello **Silver Belle**!" chimed **Elf Cinnamon Twist**, as he crossed her path with a long-winded list.

"I'm looking for Santa's special treat, without this last piece it just won't be complete! If I don't find it soon the surprise could be spoiled! **Mrs. Claus** and the others have endlessly toiled. **Cinnamon Twist**, with your keen eyes did anything strange here happen to arise?"

All the elf did was shake his head, but gave Silver Belle a few encouraging words instead.

"I'm sorry to say there's been nothing to see, and haven't a clue of where they may be. All things here are smooth sailing, even with all the letters children are mailing. Now when I'm in a pickle and at my wits end, the best thing I do is to turn to a friend. Who knows sweets better than sweet **Sugar Belle**? I'm sure she can find where the missing treats dwell. I heard she just got back from the **Peppermint Sea**, so down by the harbor is where she will be."

winter

Then off he went, with more work to do. But his words stuck around, because they were true. With no cookies here as it would seem, it was off to the next stop to uncover this sugary scheme. With a sigh **Silver Belle** turned to the best friend she could. If she couldn't find the gingerbreads, then her sister surely would. Down to the docks **Silver Belle** raced, finding her sister in the predicted place. With flour and frosting all over her face she wasn't shy to give **Silver Belle** a loving embrace.

“I need your help to solve this folly, without this surprise **Santa’s party** just won’t be as jolly. While you were away past the **Peppermint Sea**, I helped in the bakery where you’d normally be. I looked away for a moment from the fresh gingerbreads, and when I looked back they were all gone instead! I’ve been searching and searching without any luck, I’m sorry to say that I’m completely stuck.”

Sugar Belle chuckled, saying don't worry. She promised to help solve this mystery, and do it in a hurry. The two flew down the cobblestone street, racing towards the toy shop on swift steady feet.

"To solve this puzzle we'll need one more clue, I have a suspicion I think just might be true. Lucky for us, I know just who to ask. No one else is better for this particular task. When you told me what happened, it gave me slight pause. So the best thing to do, is to ask **Mrs. Claus**."

So back they went, to where it all began. And although both were tired, the two sisters ran. Flying through the doors, down the halls thinking of their new plan. But when they arrived, the scene was not blue. In fact, just the opposite seemed to be true.

Silver Belle stopped and rubbed her eyes. For what happened, from what she could contrive, was that the cookies didn't simply vanish.

— they had all come alive!

"Sweet sugar snaps!" **Silver Belle** cried, for what she saw could not be denied. Each and every face was smiling and all were bright-eyed.

Mrs. Claus laughed while opening her old recipe book, then she set it down on the counter so they could all have a look.

After dusting off flour from the ever-worn pages, everyone saw what had been true through the ages.

"Don't worry sweet dear, you did nothing wrong. You did everything right by the book all along...

...For this special treat comes with a very special power, and the secret you see is in this **magical flour**. While you were so very busy whisking up all sorts of **delicious sugary** trends, you didn't even notice our new little friends."

winter

Then how they laughed, when the mystery was solved. All the suspects in question, were now all absolved. What sweet new friends for this perfect day, to dance and sing the merry night away. Sometimes good things come from unexpected ends, and who best to find them with than your ***very best friends***?

Sight Seeing with Silver Belle

While our adventure unfolds, as we set the stage. We'll need your help as you turn every page! Look very closely and sharpen your eyes, and we promise you'll uncover a magic surprise! For in this book in all sorts of places, we think you'll find some familiar faces.

- ○ A Snowman wearing a scarf
- ○ Blue and white candy canes
- ○ Silver bells on red string
- ○ A mug in every color of the rainbow
- ○ A white Ermine
- ○ Two Puffins
- ○ A cookie wearing a scarf
- ○ An Old Water Wheel
- ○ A polka dotted present
- ○ A lucky horseshoe
- ○ Rudolf the Red Nosed Reindeer
- ○ Santa's reading glasses.
- ○ Two toy horses
- ○ Mini Elf Toys
- ○ A yellow unicorn cookie
- ○ A polar bear wearing a party hat
- ○ Two rabbits
- ○ An old tortoise in a hat
- ○ Small Santa doll
- ○ A squirrel with a hat
- ○ Magical snowflakes
- ○ A yellow candy cane
- ○ A white Christmas stocking
- ○ Moose tracks in the snow

GINGERBREAD

RECIPE

Gingerbread Cookies! Makes 2½ dozen; 2½" cookies

1/3 c shortening
1 c brown sugar
1½ c. dark molasses
2/3 c. cold water
7 c. flour

2 tsp. soda
1 tsp salt
1 tsp. allspice
1 tsp ginger
1 tsp. cloves
1 tsp cinnamon

Mix shortening, sugar, & molasses. Stir in water, Blend flour and all dry ingredients, stir in & chill Heat oven to 350° Roll dough ¼" thick on floured board. Use cookie cutters - Gingerbread! Bake 10-12 minutes on lightly greased baking sheet! Enjoy! ☺

Say Hello to Silver Belle!

Scan to learn more

What the Silver Bell Means to Me

A reminder that carries
the wonders of hope & the
joy of believing.

Made in the USA
Monee, IL
21 October 2025